Doves

Doves

Mary Ann McDonald

THE CHILD'S WORLD®, INC.

Library of Congress Cataloging-in-Publication Data

McDonald, Mary Ann.
Doves / by Mary Ann McDonald.
p.   cm.
Includes index.
Summary: Describes the physical characteristics, behavior,
habitat, and life cycle of doves, including the mourning dove,
the ground dove, and the rock dove.
ISBN 1-56766-593-4 (lib. bdg. : alk paper)
1. Columbidae—Juvenile literature.
[1. Pigeons.]   I. Title.
QL696.C63M38   1999
598.6'5—dc21   98-42058
                              CIP
                              AC

Photo Credits

© A. Morris/VIREO: 29
ANIMALS ANIMALS © Carol L. Geake: 10
ANIMALS ANIMALS © Michael Habicat: 19
ANIMALS ANIMALS © Ted Levin: 16
© 1995 Anthony Mercieca/Dembinsky Photo Assoc. Inc.: 2
© Beth Davidow/WorldWild: 30
© C. K. Lorenz, The National Audubon Society Collection/Photo Researchers: 26
© Cliff Beittel: 9
© Daniel J. Cox/Natural Exposures, Inc.: 6
© 1998 Dominique Braud/Dembinsky Photo Assoc. Inc.: 20
© 1998 Lynn M. Stone: 24
© Nigel Dennis, The National Audubon Society Collection/Photo Researchers: 23
© R. J. Erwin, The National Audubon Society Collection/Photo Researchers: cover
© Rob Curtis/VIREO: 15
© Steve Maslowski, The National Audubon Society Collection/Photo Researchers: 13

On the cover...

Front cover: It is easy to see the beautiful colors in this *rock dove's* feathers.
Page 2: This *white-winged dove* is getting ready to land on a fence post.

Table of Contents

Looking out your window on a nice summer morning, you see many little birds picking seeds out of your bird feeder. As they pick out their favorite seeds, they knock many others onto the ground. Down below, you notice a larger, gray bird cleaning up this mess in the grass. What kind of bird is this? It's a dove!

⇐ This *mourning dove* is searching the ground for food.

What Do Doves Look Like?

Doves have round bodies with small, round heads. Most have long, slender tails and are gray or brown in color. Some doves have patches of white or brown in their feathers, too.

All doves have strong wings that are covered with beautiful feathers. When they fly, they beat their wings quickly to lift them into the air. On the ground, doves use their skinny legs to walk. They take tiny steps and bob their heads as they go.

This *common ground dove* is sitting on a fence post in Texas. ⇒

Are All Doves the Same?

There are more than 250 kinds, or **species,** of doves in the world. They live almost everywhere, from city parks to country fields. In fact, the only places you won't find doves are in the far north and in very thick forests.

Not all doves look the same. The *ground dove* has a short, stubby tail. *Rock doves* have many different colors all over their bodies. The *mourning dove* is the most common dove in North America. Its softly colored feathers make it one of the most beautiful of all doves. It sings a very sad-sounding "coo, coo, coo" song.

⇐ Rock doves like this one are also called *pigeons.*

What Do Doves Eat?

Doves are ground feeders. They walk slowly along, looking for anything that looks good. Doves eat mostly seeds and grains that they find lying around. They also eat insects and snails. Since doves don't have any teeth, they must swallow all of their food whole.

To help crush the food in their stomachs, doves eat small stones and dirt, called **grit.** The grit sits inside the dove's stomach and mixes with the food the dove eats. As the food moves through the dove's body, the grit crushes it into tiny pieces.

These mourning doves are searching a snowy cornfield for food. ⇒

How Do Doves Drink?

Water is very important to doves. In dry areas, they fly great distances just to drink once a day. Most birds drink by scooping water into their beaks. They raise their heads and the water runs down their throats. Doves drink differently. They keep their heads down and suck up the water instead. In fact, the way doves drink is a lot like the way you drink through a straw.

This *white-tipped dove* is drinking from a puddle. ⇒

When they are ready to lay their eggs, most birds build strong nests of mud, twigs, and grass. Not doves! A dove's nest is very weak. It is often made of only a few sticks, a little grass, and some leaves. Instead of nesting high in trees like other birds, doves nest near the ground. They build their nests on stumps of trees, on low tree branches, and even on house ledges.

⇐ This mourning dove nest is in a pine tree in New York.

What Are Baby Doves Like?

After a pair of doves mate, the female lays one or two eggs inside the nest. Both parents take turns sitting on the eggs to keep them warm and safe. During the day, the male dove watches the eggs. At night, it's the female's turn.

In a little over two weeks, the eggs hatch. The babies, or **squabs,** are very tiny. They are blind and do not have any feathers. Over a few weeks, the squabs grow bigger and gain more feathers.

This mourning dove squab is only one week old. ⇒

Parent doves feed their squabs something called **"pigeon milk."** It is a thick fluid made from the seeds the parent has eaten. The milk is held in a special pouch in the parent's throat called a **crop.** To get the milk, the squab sticks its beak inside the parent's mouth. The parent uses its throat muscles to pump the milk into the squab's beak.

Do Doves Live in Groups?

When the squabs are grown, doves gather together into large groups called **flocks.** By living and traveling in flocks, doves stay safer than they would be alone. In a flock, one dove is always watching for danger. If an enemy tries to attack, the birds fly and flap wildly. This confuses the enemy so the doves can get away.

This flock of *cape turtle doves* is gathering at a waterhole in Africa. ⇒

Doves also gather into flocks to stay warm in cold weather. They press themselves tightly together and share the warmth from their bodies. *Inca doves* have another trick—they make pyramids to stay warm! A few birds in the flock make a row. Then more birds sit on top of them. By sitting close together like this, the doves stay much warmer than they would all by themselves.

Doves have many enemies. While they are sitting on their eggs, adult doves are sometimes attacked by squirrels, cats, snakes, raccoons, and bigger birds. Hawks and owls like to eat doves.

Doves face many other dangers, too. Very cold or very hot weather can cause doves to become sick or even die. Many doves are killed when they fly into powerlines. Others are killed when they eat things by mistake, such as poison people put out for mice.

⇐ This mourning dove may be in danger as she sits on her eggs.

Are Doves Hunted?

In many areas, doves are considered to be **songbirds.** Cardinals, wrens, sparrows, and robins are also songbirds. In many states, doves are protected. They cannot be killed or hunted by people. In other states, doves are considered to be prize game birds. They are hunted for sport and for food. These areas have strict laws that limit the number of doves people can kill each year.

Band-tailed pigeons like this one have been hunted by people. ⇒

Where Can You See Doves?

Doves are easy to attract to your backyard feeders. Spread seeds on the ground or on low platforms. Cracked corn and millet are favorite seeds for doves. The next time you go to the park, take some birdseed along. Throw some seed out on the ground near you. If rock doves are in the area, the free meal will attract them. Doves are fun to watch as they strut around, bobbing their heads back and forth. Have some fun and go feed the birds!

⇐ This rock dove is looking for food in a city park.

Glossary

crop (KROP)
A crop is a special pouch in the throat of some birds. Parent doves store "pigeon milk" in their crops for their babies.

flocks (FLOKS)
Flocks are groups of birds. Doves live together in flocks.

grit (GRIT)
Grit is the small stones and dirt that doves eat. The grit sits in the dove's stomach and helps to crush food.

pigeon milk (PIH–jen MILK)
Pigeon milk is the special fluid parent doves feed to their babies. Pigeon milk is stored in the parent's crop.

songbirds (SONG–birdz)
Songbirds are birds that make a musical call. Robins, sparrows, and doves are all songbirds.

squabs (SKWABZ)
Squabs are baby doves. Squabs are born blind and without feathers.

species (SPEE–sheez)
A species is a different kind of an animal. There are more than 250 species of doves.

Index